HOMOPHOBIC HEALER

A Primer for Gays, Lesbians and the Families and Friends Who Love Them

Sandra St. John, Ed.D.

THE
GODDESS

EXPRESS

GODDESS EXPRESS PRESS
an imprint of
Tickerwick Publications

Copyright © 1994 by Goddess Express. All rights reserved. No part of this book may be reproduced or transmitted in any form or by any means including electronic, mechanical, photocopying or by information storage and retrieval systems without written permission from the author, except for use of brief quotations.

Cover and art design © Goddess Express
First Edition
First printing 1994
Editor: Jill Klunder

Printed in the United States of America
by McNaughton & Gunn

Tickerwick Publications
P.O. Box 100695
Denver, Colorado 80250

Library of Congress Cataloging in Publication Data

St. John, Sandra, 1939-
   The homophobic healer : a primer for gays, lesbians and the families and friends who love them / Sandra St. John. -- 1. ed.
     p. cm.
   ISBN 1-885084-33-1
   1. Homosexuality--Religious aspects. 2. Gays--Life skills guides. 3. Homophobia--Treatment. 4. Gays--Prayer-books and devotions.
I. Title.
BL65.H64S7 1994
291. 1'7834766--dc20   94-23311
                                                        CIP

ACKNOWLEDGMENTS

Many individuals have contributed to the soil from which the creation of this book has come. At times, it seemed like fertilizer. True to form, the total contribution did yield a healthy plant.

My gratitude must begin with my parents for always loving, giving and being wonderful role models for the treatment of others. My father taught me many spiritual lessons through the example of his life and my mother has always inspired me through her example of unconditional love for her family.

I give thanks for those special friends who have influenced my life for the better and helped me to heal. I thank Peg and Rita for being a part of my life and enabling me to begin the healing process. I thank Bobbi for her message of importance on the "coming out" process and Helen for being there to help me through my "dark night of the soul". I thank Susan for leading me to information which allowed me to better understand my mother.

Special thanks is given to my dear friend, Connie, for her twelve step message and to my wonderful friend, Gayle, for all of her spiritual support, always being there for me and for instigating the writing of this book. I give special thanks to Blanche for being the bright light at the end of a long, dark tunnel and for sharing her life with me.

Most of all, I give thanks to God as the source of my being, the source of my strength and for God's guidance and God's willingness to use me as a vehicle for presenting these thoughts to the world. You "restoreth my Soul".

Sandra St. John
July, 1994

*This book is lovingly dedicated to
Blanche for her love, understanding and spiritual
support in my life.*

PREFACE

The experience of growing up as a "gay" person in the U.S.A. has given me the opportunity to experience the mental and emotional pain of what it means to be gay and to live a secret life. It has also provided me the opportunity to struggle with self-worth issues without knowing this was, in fact, what I was doing. The struggle was so painful it led to escape through alcohol abuse. This eventually led me to physical, emotional and financial devastation. Such a process has been referred to as the "dark night of the soul".

While I was always aware of God's presence in my life, I became more able to practice the presence of God after that time. The experience of living through the pain truly became a blessing.

My own "coming out" to my mother (my father had passed away by that time) was much delayed, and this prolonged lack of honesty deprived me of a close relationship with her for a large portion of my adult life. I shall never forget the moment of disclosure and her response: "Sandra, there isn't anything that you could do or be that could ever stop me from loving you. Because I realize how difficult this must have been for you, it only makes me love you more." My only regret about coming out is not doing it sooner.

The Homophobic Healer is about the things I have learned and found to be of value on my journey toward wholeness. I am still diligently working on this process. I offer these ideas as a path toward wholeness for all gays, lesbians, their families and friends. The older ones can use it for damage control and the younger ones can use it to avoid the mistakes of the past.

Take what you can of these ideas and implement them in your life. If they work for you, make a commitment to give them away to others through your example. If you are empowered, it is your responsibility to empower others. This is how the world will heal.

CONTENTS

Chapter 1	HOMOPHOBIA	1
Chapter 2	TO BE OR NOT TO BE	10
Chapter 3	THE CART BEFORE THE HORSE	17
Chapter 4	CREATE A WORK OF ART	21
Chapter 5	YOUR THOUGHTS CREATE YOUR WORLD	27
Chapter 6	YOU CAN HAVE WHATEVER YOU WANT	37
Chapter 7	THE PATH TO GOD	46
Chapter 8	PERSONAL HEALING: FORGIVENESS IS THE KEY	54
Chapter 9	BALANCE	63
Chapter 10	ESPECIALLY FOR PARENTS, FRIENDS AND EMPLOYERS	70
Chapter 11	COMING OUT HELPS EVERYONE TO HEAL	83
Chapter 12	A NEW BEGINNING	89
Appendix	SERVICES OFFERED THROUGH THE GODDESS EXPRESS	93

Chapter 1

HOMOPHOBIA

The author shall define homophobia as any thought or action regarding homosexuality which is based in fear, guilt or judgment. It is safe to conclude, to some degree, most persons are homophobic. The ideas presented in this book allow the reader to examine his or her own belief system regarding homosexuality and to heal the aspects of it which stand as barriers to love and acceptance of self and others.

An example of a fear-based thought which is not uncommon among heterosexuals whom are homophobic is: "Homosexuals are sexually dangerous to my children". This is an irrational thought because it assumes that all homosexuals are unconscionable. It is not rational to assume that an entire group of people is without a conscience or a sense of propriety. This is as irrational as it would be to suggest: "Heterosexuals are sexually dangerous to my children". Contemplating the latter fear enables one to see how ridiculous is the former fear. The truth is that neither homosexuals nor heterosexuals are sexually dangerous to children unless they are unconscionable individuals.

It should be recognized that there are aberrant personalities within both groups. While it may be natural to fear the aberrant personalities of both groups, it is not rational to assume that all members of either group have identical characteristics of a negative or positive nature. Both groups have their share of deviants. In fact, the truth of the matter is that the majority of child molestations are perpetuated by heterosexuals. To assume this says their propensity for sexual abuse is also greater simply because their numbers are higher, is also irrational.

That homosexuals, as a group, are sexually dangerous to anyone's children is equally irrational. This thought, however, is commonly held by heterosexuals who are homophobic. All irrational thoughts are in need of healing if the thinker would be whole.

Homophobia is not a condition which only affects heterosexuals. Homosexuals are equally homophobic although the manifestations of their homophobia are quite different from heterosexuals.

An example of a fear-based thought commonly held by a homophobic homosexual is: "If they find out I am gay or lesbian, it will negate all of my good qualities and contributions and they shall reject me." Is it not also irrational to believe that an entire of group of people would reject a person because of one aspect of their nature? If one is a good person who treats others well and contributes to the world in a positive manner, what is there to reject? Maintaining this fear ascribes to heterosexuals, as a group, the identical characteristic of irrationality they have ascribed to homosexuals. The same problem exists for each group in relation to the other.

Homophobia becomes a method by which both groups underestimate the other. It is a way for each group to distance themselves from each other and to thus avoid understanding the truth of the matter which is that they are both acting irrationally.

The majority of homosexuals have been content to exist as a silent minority and this has created the conditions which exist today. Many heterosexuals must put a mythical face on homosexuality because they believe they do not know any homosexuals. If the homosexuals they know and admire would so identify themselves, they would be able to have a different opinion on the subject and to see it as it is, one area of individual difference. The conditions of prejudice cannot change until silence becomes disclosure. Until then, heterosexuals must continue to fear the unknown because they do not know who these good people are.

Once disclosure has taken place, there shall be a time of profound communication which will lead to a different understanding. This shall lead to a cleansing of belief systems and the world shall heal. The length of time for cleansing is relative to the amount of time it takes for silence to become sound. If every gay and lesbian would reveal their nature today to every significant person in their life, the world would see the value of these individuals, the significance of their contributions and this would enable both groups to release their fears. "How can I be afraid of you when you have always been my dearest friend?"

When the heterosexual population can see that the doctor who has been treating their family for years is homosexual, that some of the best teachers in their educational system are gay or lesbian, that their stock broker, maid, banker, electrician, beautician, friends, family members and even their own children are gay or lesbian, only then will their fears be able to be released. These are persons they already know, love and trust. It is through such knowledge that heterosexuals shall release their homophobic fears and it is through the provision of such personal knowledge to the world that homosexuals shall heal their own homophobia.

It is the belief of the author that homosexuality does not come about because of a conscious choice made by the homosexual after they are born, but rather that this aspect of their being is an inherent part of their nature. For whatever reasons the soul has for personal healing and God has for their soul growth, it is part of *The Plan* for them to express as a homosexual. One might consider, homophobia, as felt and experienced in the world, may be viewed as a lack of faith in God's plan and as a rejection of it. It seems proper to recognize that any individual, organization, church or state who speaks with a voice of hate that is born of fear is not speaking for a loving God nor are they accepting of God's creations.

God created all that exists. God created African Americans. God created handicapped individuals. God created women. God created old people. God created homosexuals. Could the purpose have been so that a large segment of the population could become their most biased, bigoted and righteous selves? Could the purpose have been to perpetuate fear, hate and oppression of others? One does not have to be a rocket scientist to see that the answer is "No"; however, each reader must make their own decisions on this. They must also live by the consequences of them.

We know that we reap what we sow. Humanity cannot afford to sow anything less than expressions which are loving and accepting of all humanity regardless of differences such as race, color, gender, age and sexual orientation. Our constitution demands it and God expects it.

As every gay, lesbian, their families and friends begin to understand and heal their irrational homophobic thoughts, the world can more deeply experience the love of God in the world. It is to this end that homophobia will be more carefully examined.

Like all phobias, homophobia is fear-based. Being homophobic is to be afraid of homosexuality. While there is nothing to fear, it is a natural thing to fear the unknown. Fear is often an indication that additional knowledge is needed. For instance, if you were asleep and you were awakened by a noise, you might become fearful that someone has broken into your home. If you were to get up, go into the kitchen and discover that your cat knocked over a candlestick while prowling about, you would be able to release your fears about the situation. The additional knowledge would release your fear. Likewise, if you knew your gay and lesbian friends as homosexual, this would help you to release your fears regarding homosexuality.

Heterosexuals and homosexuals are both homophobic for different reasons. Both groups need additional information to release their fears. Each group enters the world with a human race memory which was precipitated by mankind's initial preoccupation with procreation of the species. Race memory is defined here as the remembrance of emotionally charged ideas which are handed down from generation to generation. Both groups are further conditioned by their parents, some churches and society in general to believe that homosexuality is wrong. The reality is that all exists exactly as God created it, that we have been counseled by a loving God not to be judgmental of others and we have failed.

Parents and churches tend to condition as they were conditioned. They tend to believe what they were taught. It is quite understandable and it makes them neither right nor wrong. The point here is that once upon a time, people were taught that the world was flat. They believed it until additional knowledge proved that belief to be incorrect. Because of the prevailing irrational thoughts about homosexuality, it is no wonder both heterosexuals and homosexuals are homophobic. It is time for all of us to heal.

There is no one more confused than a gay or lesbian child. Many realize their nature at a very early age. They are as God created them and somehow this seems to be unacceptable to the world. It is very confusing. They easily come to believe that selective secrecy will somehow protect and keep them from harm. They seek out protection from their fears of rejection and they learn not to live openly as homosexuals. It is what is known as living "in the closet". This is extremely detrimental to their self acceptance and to their self esteem.

A parallel can be drawn here between closeted gays and lesbians and those who have been sexually abused and silently carry their burden. Just as the sexually abused person is able to heal by sharing their burden with others and confronting the issue, the closeted gay and lesbian can also heal through communication with others. We are only as sick as our deepest, darkest secret.

The additional knowledge needed by gays and lesbians to resolve their fears is simple but often elusive. They must first accept themselves as God created them and love themselves for the wonderful persons they are. Until they are able to accept God's will with regard to their nature and love themselves, they are unable to unconditionally love others.

Their will and God's will is ONE. Accepting this discovery is one of life's most important lessons. Living this additional knowledge through action is all that is needed for the gay and lesbian to release their homophobic fears. Afraid no more of who they are, gays and lesbians shall refuse to live in the closet.

Releasing their fears will enable them to experience all of life as the gay or lesbian they are. If they are to live a life of honesty, the older gays and lesbians must come out of the closet once and for all and the younger gays and lesbians must not create a closet in the first place.

By claiming the freedom to be who they are, homosexual persons remove the barriers to intimacy with their parents, friends, employers and significant others. There are no big secrets about their homosexuality worth keeping. This allows everyone to heal.

Heterosexuals also need additional knowledge so that they can heal their homophobia. Most of them have no idea of how many homosexuals they already know and love. When they realize they know, like, love and admire many individuals they never before recognized as lesbian or gay, healing shall begin. This kind of openness will allow heterosexuals to love even more deeply and compassionately because their homosexual friend cared enough to trust them.

Most persons will be loving and supportive. The ones who cannot be loving and supportive have issues of their own to heal. Such a revelation will often help them in doing so. Openness, honesty and willingness to communicate always facilitates the healing process. It is possible for the world to heal homophobia but it cannot come to pass until gays and lesbians come out of the closet.

This brings us back to the old saying: "Which came first, the chicken or the egg?" Homosexuals may say: "Because the world is homophobic, I have to live in the closet." The truth of the matter is: as long as gays and lesbians continue to live in the closet, the world will remain homophobic.

REFLECTIONS

Mother-Father God, give me the understanding and acceptance to know You are a loving God who created me the way I am for a purpose. I shall do my part to end homophobia in the world.

It all must start with me and I am willing to heal. I am willing to love and accept myself exactly as You created me. Because Your spark of Divinity is within me, loving myself is not unrelated to loving You. Help me to more fully express You in the world. Help me to only love and only give.

The world wants to heal around judgment. Help me to do my part and avoid the judgment of others no matter what they may say or do. Help me to understand that all any human being is trying to do is heal. Help me to be a catalyst in the healing process for all people.

I know that You are always with me. When I close my eyes and call to You, Your comforting words and Your guidance are there. I give thanks for Your presence in my life.

Chapter 2

TO BE OR NOT TO BE

There exists a great deal of misunderstanding in the world on what it means to be gay or lesbian and how an individual arrives at such a destination. "Are they born this way or does their environment condition them to become gay or lesbian?" Interesting ideas may be offered to support either opinion but there is not a way to win the argument that one belief is right and the other is wrong. The ideas presented in this book emanate from a much larger perspective which in turn supports both points of view.

There is only God. There is a power greater than ourselves and all that exists in the world is part of God's creation. All creations are part of God, yet God is more than any one creation or the sum of all of them. All living creatures have a spark of God's divinity within them which establishes their interconnectedness. We are all part of each other and we are all part of God. To learn to experience this Oneness is why we are here.

There is no will but God's. We are here to make the profound discovery that our will and God's will are one. We are here to learn the truth about God, that God only loves and gives. We are here to learn to become more God-like, first in our thoughts, then through our actions in the world.

Life as we know it is but a series of lessons in God's school of learning to teach us to love and to give unconditionally. How well we are learning these lessons can be measured by the extent of our anger, the amount of our judgment against others, our reluctance to forgive, our unwillingness to accept God's will, the lack of peace we feel within ourselves, and every thought and deed that is not loving or giving. Homophobia is only one of the many challenges which shows us how far we still have to go to heal.

Because there is only God and God's will, being gay and lesbian is a part of God's plan for these individuals. They are born gay or lesbian into the environment which their soul selects with God to best allow them the opportunity for healing expression. This environment allows for the nurturing of their nature.

The only choice a gay or lesbian has regarding their status is whether they choose to express or to suppress their nature and to what degree. Gay and lesbian is who they are. Mommy and daddy did not do anything wrong in their upbringing to create this reality. This is God's will for them. The lack of willingness, by themselves and others, to accept God's will is at the very core of homophobia.

When a gay or lesbian chooses to fully express who they are, they are flowing in acceptance with God's will for them. They will be learning the lessons God intends for them to learn. By doing so, they are playing their part in God's plan and only good will come from it. In fully expressing who they are, they will come out to their parents, their friends and later, to their employers. In the process, they become totally accepting of who they are and thus, emotionally healthier individuals. This also permits others to more easily accept them for who they are. This allows both the gay and lesbian, their family, friends and employers to heal their homophobia.

One reason the world has not healed on the issue of homophobia is because gays and lesbians have chosen not to fully express who they are. Because they have been unwilling to fully play their part in God's plan, they have disallowed the world to heal it's prejudice about them. Homophobia will continue to exist only as long as gays and lesbians continue to remain in the closet.

If every gay and lesbian person would begin to express who they are to all the significant people in their life, the world would indeed have an opportunity to see they are productive members of society, and are basically good people who contribute greatly to making this world a better place. Gays and lesbians are doctors, lawyers, teachers, artist, carpenters, electricians, secretaries and sales persons. They are represented in all walks of life and their contributions are broad and substantial.

Most importantly, if they fully expressed who they are, the world would see that gays and lesbians are a part of every family. It is commonly accepted that one in ten persons are homosexual. This gives to each family the potential of having a homosexual member present in the not-so-distant family progression. Because loving relationships usually already exist within the family, they can play an important role in helping gays, lesbians and their families to heal. As families help their members to heal, they also heal their own homophobia.

It is not easy to be gay in this society. Essentially, gays and lesbians want the same things everyone else wants; they want to be loved and accepted for who they are. Because they have grown up in a homophobic society, they fear rejection in expressing who they are and this precipitates a need to suppress their nature.

In doing so, many times gays and lesbians will marry in flight from themselves. This often creates much emotional pain in their lives as they desperately try to be something they are not. This also adds to the emotional pain of others. Suppression rarely works for a lifetime.

Other individuals who suppress their nature to the point of total denial, are able to do so only by projecting onto the homosexual world the personal conflict with which they are unable to cope. They project their bias and anger onto others in order to avoid dealing with it from a personal perspective. They become the gay bashers, the righteous zealots and in general, those who are only willing to accept God's will selectively through their own interpretation. They are the homophobics most in need of healing.

What seems to be the case most often is that gays and lesbians accept and express their nature in limited ways. Some are out only to their lover and a few gay friends. Some are out to their parents and some are not. Some are "out" at work. Most are not. One thing that gays and lesbians who choose limited expression have in common is the issue of control. They often find themselves exerting a great deal of it to achieve their goal of selective secrecy. In the process, they often become control freaks while living a life which is basically dishonest. One would not choose to live dishonestly if the prevailing feeling were: "I'm OK".

This group of gays and lesbians has high occurrences of drug and alcohol abuse. Such abuse assists the individual in the escaping of feelings. The addiction thus stymies the emotional growth of the addicted. Drug and alcohol rehabilitation enables feelings to surface and by doing so, the individual can begin the healing process. Personal healing always brings a greater understanding and acceptance of the self. This understanding often leads to a greater expression of the nature of self which, in this case, is gay or lesbian and precipitates an expansion of the coming out process.

Even if addiction is not a part of the life experience of gays and lesbians who allow only limited expression of their nature, they still suffer from the dishonesty with which they live their lives. They do not walk hand in hand on the beach enjoying the sunset with their spouse, take their spouse to the company Christmas party or acknowledge the importance of their significant other to the world. Some gays or lesbians make their home a prison for their life together. A limited expression of a homosexual nature is always emotionally damaging to the gay and lesbian.

There is no conscious choice in "to be or not to be" gay or lesbian. Being born with a homosexual nature is part of God's plan. The choice in the matter revolves around whether or not the individual chooses to accept God's will and how they choose to express or suppress their nature. Whatever their choice happens to be, gay is who they are.

REFLECTIONS

Help me Mother-Father God to become more accepting of all persons and to know that all which exists is part of Your plan so each one of us can be healed. As we become so, we lay down our anger and judgment. We become more loving and giving to all. We feel only peace within and we express only peace in the world.

Help everyone to realize their interconnectedness. To hate another is to hate oneself and You. To love another is to love oneself and You. Help us to experience our Oneness with You and with all that is, and to always know that the measure of our progress is how we treat others.

Chapter 3

THE CART BEFORE THE HORSE

It is commendable that gay activists are willing to work for beneficial change in the human rights arena. In many states, activists are fighting various initiatives which would deny basic human rights to gays and lesbians. This quest should certainly continue but the battle cannot be fully won until the gay and lesbian community is willing to be supportive by standing up, being counted and living without apology for who they are.

The "March on Washington" is the symbol for gays and lesbians feeling good about themselves in this regard. It would indeed be healthy for this feeling to be extended into every city and town. Let there be a "Gay March" on Atlanta, New York, Tampa, Denver, Portland, Los Angeles, Miami and everywhere in the U.S.A. Only when gays and lesbians are willing to stand up and be counted will they truly support the activists who work for change on their behalf.

The battle also cannot be won without heterosexuals healing their homophobia. Those who are spiritually clear would oppress no one for they shall emulate God, who only loves and gives. In fact, they would join the "March" to voice their support for human rights for gays, lesbians and all people.

If every gay, lesbian, their families and friends would come out of the closet, proclaim who they are and stand up for human rights, everyone would be standing up. Gay and lesbian rights could not help but prevail. Implementing this one thought through action would change the world as we know it.

When people begin to heal their homophobia, their consciousness will change. When their consciousness changes, they shall think differently. Those thoughts will produce different actions and different results.

The fact that President Bill Clinton went to Washington with an agenda that included gays in the military indicates that he has done a lot of healing of his homophobia and his consciousness has changed. The fact he was not successful with acceptable change on this issue speaks to the fact that the consciousness of the majority of the congressional body has not changed. Since they are the voice of their constituency, we can further assume the consciousness of the majority of those individuals also has not changed.

When consciousness changes, people will begin to heal their homophobic thoughts. They will think differently and they will speak and act differently. Changing our consciousness and healing our homophobia is "putting the horse before the cart". Only then can the issue of human rights for gays and lesbians and indeed, for all people, change. Because mass consciousness has not yet sufficiently changed, the struggle of this oppressed group continues. It is also why so many valiant efforts of the past have failed.

The author finds it interesting to note that for as long as mass consciousness has not sufficiently changed to enable equal rights for gays and lesbians, the vast majority of gays and lesbians have lived in the closet. Does it not make sense to think that coming out of the closet would have the greatest impact on bringing about this change in consciousness? It has not yet been tried and it is reasonable to think this last frontier is the only action which will bring significant and lasting results in this arena.

Such a change in consciousness will be strengthened by everyone becoming aware of the fact they know so many intelligent, nurturing and contributing members of our society to be gay or lesbian. As parents, families and friends of gays and lesbians publicly take pride in their accomplishments, and gays and lesbians take public pride in being who they are, race memory will be changed forever.

REFLECTIONS

I have the courage to move through the fears that these ideas represent for me and for my family members, friends and employers. I feel in my heart the truth about how consciousness will change and I know what I must do to play my part. I am willing to do so for "Thou art with me".

Mother-Father God, give me the guidance, wisdom and strength to love myself exactly as You created me and to express Your love in the world. I know that my strength will help others to be strong and that the world will always mirror back to me what I give out. Guide me in this process as I courageously go forward as the person You created.

Help me God to assist others in this process of healing. Help me to communicate and always share all that I know with those in need. Help me to love unconditionally and to give of myself to make this world a better place because I have passed this way.

Chapter 4

CREATE A WORK OF ART

There are basically two ways to look at life as the individual experiences the world. One is that things are basically happening by accident and that life becomes a series of reactions to the accidents that happen. This way of viewing the world is not unpopular today, as evidenced by the victim consciousness which is currently prevailing in the courts of law. "I am not responsible for my actions because thus and so was done to me".

Another way to view life is that it is created by specific design and therefore, there are no accidents. This view of the world is more predominately held by successful people. Life for them is created by the decisions they make and is brought into reality through their actions. This usually implies a goal setting process. Here, the individual assumes responsibility for the outcome.

If you were to use the analogy of a game of billiards, you could compare the first individual who "is not responsible" to the billiard balls. This person is merely acted upon by the cue ball who becomes the devil who made them do it. The other individual who assumes responsibility for the outcome of his or her life does indeed become the cue ball who makes things happen. While it is up to each individual to decide which idea to hold true about life's modus operandi, the individual must also be willing to accept responsibility for what their choices bring forth.

If one chooses to believe that life is a series of reactions to the accidents that happen, life will provide the possibility that many things will happen for which the individual need never be responsible. Since the person is not responsible for what happens, blame is always placed on something or someone else. Such a belief system is very disempowering because there is always something or someone else who is in the driver's seat of their life.

On the other hand, it is very empowering to subscribe to the belief that life is not happening by accident but rather that it is being purposely created. This implies ownership and responsibility. This individual is indeed in the driver's seat of their life.

It appears that most human beings do not exclusively subscribe to one view of life in application to their own life's experience. Most seem to apply one view to some parts of their life's experience and the opposing view to other parts. For instance, a person may be a "cue ball" with regard to making things happen in their professional life and they may abandon that role to become the reactive "billiard balls" when it comes to their personal life. Their emotional life may have one application while their spiritual life ascribes to the other view. The success of a life may very well be determined by the percentage of the life ascribing to the "cue ball" empowered belief system. The higher this percentage, the more successful is the life.

With few exceptions, gays and lesbians experience the part of their lives that is their homosexuality in the reactive, disempowered mode of the "billiard balls" belief system. Living "in the closet" is merely an extension of this belief. To believe that one can make a positive and a successful statement of honestly owning their life as a gay or lesbian person, displays an adherence to an empowering "cue ball" system of belief.

As you examine which areas of your life you are in the driver's seat of empowerment, it may also be helpful for you to examine your feelings of aloneness. If you believe that you are alone in the process of life creation, you can still accomplish great things. As you do so, however, you may also experience an unidentified loneliness. You are accomplishing things but it somehow feels empty. If you recognize, seek and accept God's help in life, you can create a partnership of power which knows no limitations.

Being a child of God, each individual has God within them. The relationship of a child to their parents is similar to the relationship of an individual to Mother-Father God. No one is ever separated from God, even though it may sometimes feel that way, any more than one can ever be completely separated from their parents. They are and shall forever be from them. They have genetic likeness, similar physical appearance and sometimes, mannerisms which are very reflective of their parents.

You can never be separated from God because you are of God. This spark of Divinity within can be described as your spiritual genetics. It is the team of you and God who best creates a meaningful life.

God may be likened to the playwright who conceives the idea and the outline for the soul's growth. The idea and the outline would include the time of birth and to whom the individual is born, and all of the major events and significant people in our life, as well as the time of our death.

Your part in this creative duo is that of an actor or actress who creates the dialogue and movement which give detail to the outline. While you are creating this detail of thought and action, God is always available as a drama coach. While help is available, it is not mandatory that it be accepted. If you would rather do it yourself, this is perfectly acceptable to God. If you should stumble and decide to change your mind about God's help, this is also perfectly acceptable.

The quality of the play depends upon the choices made by you relative to dialogue and movement. The quality of your life depends upon how well you write the play. Will it win a Tony or will it be just another play which also ran? The choice rests with you.

So many gays and lesbians are not at all accepting of the outline into which their homosexuality has been written. It is not an easy lifestyle to live; every gay and lesbian has at sometime in their life wished that this were not their burden to carry.

Time spent on such contemplation is not productive because it cannot change the outline God created. God has very specific reasons for the outline of each individual drama. Being willing to accept God's will with regard to the outline is where the acceptance process must begin. Unfortunately, it is not uncommon for many gays and lesbians to spend much of their life fighting a battle which cannot be won yet is most certainly lost through the lack of acceptance of the nature of self and God.

The moral of this story is: **DO NOT FIGHT THE OUTLINE.** Accept God's will and know that only good shall come of it, even when such good is not readily apparent. Know that God is always there to help, to love and to give. Open your heart now and enter your powerful partnership with God.

Resolve to develop the outline in the most beautiful and meaningful manner possible. Resolve to create a work of art.

REFLECTIONS

Help me to create of my life a work of art which is inspirational to all. You have given me the perfect outline and a creative heart with unlimited potential. Help me to live my part in life's drama in Your name, so that my dialogue praises You and my actions emulate You. This is my heart's desire.

Mother-Father God, help me to reach out to those who would oppress me out of fear and let them see my face in the light so we can heal. Help me to know that forgiveness offers me all that You have promised. I am ready for Your gifts. I am willing to forgive myself for my lack of faith in my fellow human beings and I am willing to forgive the world.

Chapter 5

YOUR THOUGHTS CREATE YOUR WORLD

Have you ever stopped to realize that your life exists exactly as you have created it to be? A gay or lesbian person may ask: "What, you mean I am responsible for the bigotry and hatred that exists against homosexuals in the world?" The answer more clearly lies in the fact that you are responsible for the bigotry and hatred that exists in your world. How intolerant are you of your lifestyle? How accepting are you of your homosexual life? How much do you love yourself? The answers to these questions have everything to do with what a gay or lesbian person experiences in their world. If it exists in their life, they have created it.

Accepting the blessing of this responsibility is indeed empowering. Because you are the creator of all that exists in your world, you can change it at any time you choose. The things you do not like about your world are but the mere reflection of the things you do not like about yourself.

How do you feel about your treatment in the world? Does the world treat you fairly? If not, this may suggest that you do not feel worthy of fair treatment. If this is so, then it would follow that you would place yourself in situations where you would experience unfair treatment. You can only experience in the world the thoughts you think about yourself. So, what kind of thoughts have you been thinking? What kind of evidence have you been gathering? If the evidence is undesirable, you might consider changing the thoughts which created it.

Changing your thoughts about yourself always creates a world which reflects differently. If a gay or lesbian is truly loving and accepting of themselves as a homosexual, this love and acceptance would reflect as love and acceptance in their world. Choosing not to live openly as the gay or lesbian that one is, or living in the closet is but a visual symbol of a lack of self love and acceptance.

When an individual becomes consciously responsible for the creation of their life, they will stop blaming others. Their parents are not to blame for bringing them into the world. Their spouse or their significant other is not to blame for the problems in their relationship. Their employer is not to blame for their lack of performance on the job. Blame becomes individual responsibility and a willingness to accept it fully and correct the errors of the past. To believe that one's life is exactly as one has created it to be is the most empowering thought a person can contemplate. If they created it, they can change it.

Let us project, for a moment, that this realization is there. After accepting responsibility for life's creation, how does one go about making the changes they desire and refining this process? In answering this question, we shall begin by investigating the idea that: ALL THINGS ARE FIRST CREATED IN MIND.

Here is an example of how this works. I have a thought that I am hungry. After having had this thought, I go to the refrigerator to see what there is to eat. It is improbable that I would find myself with a drumstick in my hand without first having had the initial thought that I am hungry. The thought allows the fulfillment of the action. The thought moves through a vehicle of expression to be fulfilled through action and resolution occurs. The process can be observed in the following manner.

THOUGHT	EXPRESSION	ACTION
I am hungry	Go to refrigerator, see availability, select	Eat

It is realistic to accept that life is created in this manner and that action in the world emanates from thought.

Let us now look at another example. I have the thought that I am sleepy. This thought precipitates my getting ready for bed and reclining which culminates in sleep. In other words, the thought suggests the vehicle for expression which then creates the action of sleep.

THOUGHT	EXPRESSION	ACTION
I am sleepy	Get ready for bed, recline	Sleep

This is the way a person creates a life experience, by a series of thoughts which move through expression to become actions in the world. The perception of our reality is colored by our feelings about the thoughts we have initiated.

As you apply this procedure to your thoughts, you will quickly see how your use of this procedure has created the world which you experience. We live in an ordered world where things do not happen by accident. Actions cannot take place in the world without being first precipitated by thought. While thoughts may be experienced at a subconscious as well as a conscious level, it is not the purpose of this book to explore subconscious motivations. Handling the conscious thoughts is mind boggling enough for most individuals.

From our previous examples, you can see how the thought must come first before expression becomes apparent to then complete the action. You can also see how the completion of the action brings about resolution and satisfaction.

All of life seeks resolution. The very fact of thought seeking expression through action is the creative process. It is as evident in music, art and drama as it is in life itself.

The other side of this condition is that when our thoughts are denied expression and are therefore not completed through action, they bring about the opposite result of frustration and dissatisfaction. They can also bring about a myriad of stress disorders and disease. Thoughts which are fear, shame or guilt based fit into this category. Let us now apply this idea to an unproductive thought not uncommon to the gay or lesbian. "I am afraid that my parents will find out I am gay". This is a thought that most every gay and lesbian person has contemplated at some time in their life.

THOUGHT   EXPRESSION   ACTION

I am afraid my parents
will find out I am gay

Notice that this thought is fear, shame and/or guilt-based. Because this is so, the gay or lesbian does not want to express this thought nor desire to take action upon it. For as long as this is so, there can be no resolution on this issue. But why, we might ask is the thought fear-based to begin with? Why is it not O.K. to be gay? The author suggests this idea has its beginning with mankind's procreation fears. Such fears have been handed down from generation to generation. Are these not irrational fears? The author believes they are. It is also wonderful to know that all fear-based thoughts can be changed.

When a thought continues to exist for which the individual continues to choose to deny expression, the thought will compound itself. As it continues to become larger and larger, it allows the thinker to feel more and more fear, shame and/or guilt. The failure to resolve thought through lack of expression and action can only produce frustration. In time, the gay or lesbian must do one of two things. They must bite the bullet and move through their fear to honestly express the thought through action. This allows them to work through the healing process with their parents. Failing to do this, they try to stymie the growth of this fast growing cancerous thought through avenues of rationalization and projection.

"My parents could not possibly handle this if I told them. Believe me, they do not want to know. They are too old to deal with this." This allows the individual to transfer their problem to their parents and to further blame the homophobic world for their dilemma. Lack of action does not allow the individual or their parents to heal. The closet thus becomes a disempowering reality which fails to solve the problem. It does not solve the problem of the gay or lesbian and it does not solve the problems of their parents in coming to terms with reality. The closet merely denies there is a problem and at great cost to the gay or lesbian.

The real issue at hand is that gay or lesbian is who they are and that they are unaccepting of their nature. This is the life which God has given them to live. Perhaps God's reasons for giving them this life have as much to do with allowing others to heal their homophobia as they do with the individual being gay or lesbian. Accepting who they are enables them to play their part in God's big picture.

Choose now to play your part by becoming the beautiful blue sky in the landscape painting that God has made. Choose freedom. With honesty, choose acceptance of who you are, a perfect child of God. If you do not believe that you are a perfect child of God, ask your mother. She knows, without a doubt, that you are. This world can only wait for you to heal your wounds of unacceptance.

There is but one modus operandi in life for everyone. Our thoughts create our life. We can consciously use the process to create a better life or we can use the process unproductively to create a life of pain. Life itself is but an elaborate drama for the materialization of the mental energy our thoughts create. Thoughts are the real creative power in the world.

It is time for every gay and lesbian to reflect upon the thoughts they hold about their homosexuality. If these thoughts are based in fear, shame and/or guilt, they can only create a life of personal pain. Reflect upon the fact that the only reason you would think a fear or shame based thought about your nature is because this is the way you have been taught. Your parents have perpetuated this belief because this is how they were taught. Is this reason enough to be absolutely certain it is correct? Is the world still flat?

This is an important dialogue for every gay and lesbian to be having with themselves. If they conclude they do not value the personal pain inflicted by their fear-based thoughts about their homosexuality, they have the power to change the thoughts which have produced them. This change will come about through choosing to express and take action upon the fear-based thought.

If the fear-based thought regarding their nature happens to be: "I am afraid my parents will find out I am gay", the individual must be willing to take a risk and move through the fear which surrounds this thought by telling their parents the truth about who they are. This may be frightening for some individuals to contemplate, but by moving through this fear, they shall change this fear-based thought forever. A healing process can then begin to take place for all concerned.

This is true for every other fear-based thought a gay or lesbian may have regarding lack of acceptance of their homosexual nature. In every situation or setting where one is uncomfortable about being known as a gay or lesbian, one must move through the fear to detach it from the thought. It is only your fears that have withheld your freedom. While today's homosexuals are not totally responsible for the initial creation of homophobia, they are completely responsible for its continuation. Always remember that thought creates the world. Your thoughts create your world. If you choose to avoid control of the process, without a doubt, it will control you.

The world is truly desirous of healing its homophobia. Even those who shout the loudest forms of condemnation from the religious right are seeking balance within their mind, heart and soul that would allow them to remove their barriers to love and acceptance of all mankind. Yes, all the world truly wants to heal their homophobia but this cannot come to be until every gay and lesbian is willing to accept themselves with love. The question continues to be: Are you willing to take a personal risk to bring about beneficial change? The entire world is depending on you. Are you willing to help the world to heal?

REFLECTIONS

Mother-Father God, grant me the vision to always see the truth as You unveil it for me and the strength to act upon it. I know that when times are difficult, You will be there to comfort and guide me. My cup runneth over.

Help me to realize that You have made no mistakes, nor have I. Help me to know that I am exactly as You created me. I am Your beautiful child who is well loved. Help me to use Your love as my model for self love. As I learn to love myself, I shall live as an example of Your love in the world. I shall help all others to heal as I heal through love, empathy and laughter. I shall heal my adversaries by refusing to hate them or to be judgmental about them. Only the God in me shall meet the God in them.

Help me Mother-Father God to release my fear based thoughts as only I can. I shall know the amount of my progress by the measure of peace that I feel inside. Bless my parents, my friends and foes as all of us progress in our understanding of each other and in our capacity to love unconditionally. For these wonderful blessings, I give thanks.

Chapter 6

YOU CAN HAVE WHATEVER YOU WANT

Assuming you have appreciation for the "cue ball philosophy" of operating in the world and an understanding of how your thoughts create your world, how exactly do you go about claiming what you want? You must know what you want before you can create it. Sometimes, looking at what you do not want can help you to arrive at this awareness.

A logical place to begin is to analytically look at the life you have and evaluate it based upon how you feel about it. Since much of the life experience revolves around relationships and money, these become excellent areas on which to focus. After all, if you were to ask your friends, "What are your dissatisfactions about your life; what is it that you really want?", do you not suspect that the answer would have something to do with relationships and money? Perhaps their relationships are not all they desire them to be. Perhaps money, and the things that money buys, is not sufficiently abundant.

If these areas are half-way satisfying, the attention may be more drawn to areas of contribution to the world. An exception to this might be the response of artistic persons or those heavily immersed in actively using the creative process. Their answer to what is important in their life may be first associated with their work, and after that to areas of relationships and money. Realizing that generalizations may always be dispelled by individual differences, it is easy to accept that most individuals want more of relationships, money and their contributions to the world.

The belief that God must provide these things is where the process seems to break down. In holding this belief, the individual leaves themself out of the process. Each person has God's spark of Divinity within themselves. It is plausible to believe that God's intention might be that one use this spark of Divinity to function as a co-creator with God in the creation of everything one desires.

Because there is a little bit of God in each of us, a conclusion might be made that there is also a little bit of us in God. This might further lead to the conclusion that God does not want to be asked to do all of the work. God just might prefer that you and God do this together. What a concept!

As one reflects upon the analysis and evaluation of the life one is living, perhaps this should also be a part of the reflection: "Have I tried to do this alone? Do I feel that God has somehow failed me?" If one has been asking God to do all of the work, it would be quite natural to feel let down in the process. This leads the individual to a belief that they have had to do this thing called life all alone and that perhaps that God is undependable. Perhaps life's results are less indicative that God has failed them than they are of the individual refusing to participate with God in doing the work. Adjusting only this one facet of one's thinking and being willing to participate with God as co-creator will itself create far different results. Adjusting other facets of one's thinking will amplify those results.

If relationships are in deficit, the identical principles are functioning. Life reflects back to one that which one is. This is why the same types of things seem to go wrong in relationship after relationship. "People always take advantage of me. My boss never appreciates me." The individual must realize that all life can do is provide a picture of one's thought so that one may more fully experience the thought. If one does not like the experience, one should change the thought. It is a lot like trying on clothes. A person tries on clothes to see if they like them. "I have tried on this dress and I do not like it." If so, they are not going to purchase it. The logical conclusion would not be to buy it, take it home and continue trying it on. "Maybe I shall grow to like it better if I try it on often enough." No one is confused about the fact that this would certainly be misguided thinking, yet this is often the way most individuals operate in the world with regard to relationships. The same issues continue to surface and the same mistakes continue to happen.

You only need understand this one thing. Life can only give you what you are. Are you loving and secure within yourself? Life can then only reflect back to you with loving and secure relationships. If people are always taking advantage of you, then as difficult as it is to face, consider that you may have a consciousness to heal that would take advantage of others. Life can only reveal your consciousness in tangible form. If you do not appreciate the results you see in life's expression, you must change the thought to change the consciousness. Striving to change the effect is like trying to change a photograph. The images cannot change until the subject matter changes and a new picture is taken. You must change the cause before the effects can change. Changing cause will lead to different thought expressions which will create different results.

If one thinks loving thoughts, one's world is filled with love. If one thinks there is more than enough money for everyone to have all that they desire, one can create the experience of having enough money to fulfill their desires. It cannot be otherwise; consciousness precipitates the thought that creates the world.

Everyone has heard that it is more difficult to break bad habits than it is to begin new ones. Cleaning up unproductive thought is not easy because it has fallen into the habitual mode. The use of affirmations is extremely helpful in interrupting the process. In other words, make the desired thought into a positive statement which is then used as an affirmation. The affirmation should be repeated often and the repetition will eventually enable the consciousness to change in the desired direction. As this happens, the affirmation then becomes the thought which creates the life experience.

To aid in this process, the author has created a set of affirmation cards entitled *AFFIRMATIONS FOR*

PERSONAL HEALING which are available to the individual. Information on how to acquire the affirmation cards appears at the end of this book.

As the title of this chapter states, YOU CAN HAVE WHATEVER YOU WANT. The process of bringing your desires into manifestation is multifaceted. The following conditions should be present in using the manifestation process most effectively. The question remains: How completely are you able to place yourself in this scenario?

1. I am willing to assume and accept complete responsibility for my life. No one else is to blame.

2. I am willing to accept my position as co-creator with God to create of my life a work of art.

3. I am willing to accept that God and I can change my world. I am willing to do my part.

4. I am willing to accept that the world is always reflecting myself back to me through the thoughts I think.

5. I am willing to accept that my thoughts have created my world and my thoughts are the only things which can change my world.

6. I am willing to analyze and evaluate the effects of my life's expressions to identify the areas I wish to change.

7. I am willing to use the natural creative process of thought through expression to action in order to change my world for the better, even if it means that I must move through my fears.

8. I am willing to use an affirmation process to assist me in changing my consciousness to achieve my desired results.

9. I am willing to give thanks to God and to the God in me for all of the good I create in my life and in the world.

You are free to accept all or any part of the process. It is the author's opinion that being able to accept all of this process can more quickly bring about greater results, however, you can only begin wherever you are. Some level of acceptance will bring some results. Greater acceptance will bring greater results. Once you see that progress is taking place, this understanding can become the catalyst for greater acceptance.

The nine point process, as stated above, is a manifestation process that will work for everyone who sincerely uses it. The more belief one has in the process, the greater it will work. It is the author's hope that all individuals who read this book will courageously try it out to prove it works to change their lives for the better.

As gays, lesbians, their families and friends apply the manifestation process to their homophobic thoughts, homophobia will cease to exist for them because their consciousness on this issue will have changed. As this happens, the world will reflect differently on this issue because the world can only reflect back to them that which they are. Homophobia is nothing more than the materialization of the mental energy of homophobic thoughts.

The consciousness of gays, lesbians, their families and friends can change on this issue if each individual becomes responsible for his/her thoughts. Doing their work thoughtfully and diligently can truly change the world.

Such a realization is especially important for all of those brave individuals who work for the civil and human rights of gays and lesbians. They cannot be successful without healing their own consciousness on homophobia. As they do so, they shall come from a powerful space of love to change the world. This change will come about more quickly as every gay, lesbian, their families and friends join them in this space of love and personal responsibility.

Homosexuals need only study and learn the non-violent methods of Gandhi and Rev. Martin Luther King, Jr. on their path to freedom. If gay activists based their activities on these methods while actively using the manifestation process, and every gay, lesbian, their families and friends inwardly and outwardly support them through identical involvement, the synergy of change in thought and consciousness shall truly change the world in the twinkling of an eye.

The emphasis of gay activists on raising money to fight initiatives is a noble one, however, it will never bring about beneficial change of a lasting nature. It will only keep homosexuals on the defensive, for the scenario consists of individuals unwilling to stand up and identify themselves contributing money to change the world on their behalf. What is wrong with this picture?

Thank God for the activists who would be used to change the world and thank God for the healing of their consciousness which will make them successful in doing so. Thank God for the active participation of each and every individual who would properly support their efforts with their own consciousness change. Only then can homophobia merge with the feelings of love and acceptance of all mankind.

REFLECTIONS

Mother-Father God, help me to realize that life as it exists is not life as it must continue to remain. I can function as a co-creator with You and together, we can change the world through love.

You have given me the ability to think and this is my creative process to use wisely. I forgive myself for using this process against myself in the past and I give thanks for the knowledge that the future can be different.

The world depends on me and my willingness to create it differently. I vow to use the strength which I now feel inside to help me in the manifestation process.

Thank you, Mother-Father God, for all that I am, all that I am capable of being and all that I shall be. Your peace, Your love and Your joy go with me wherever I go and all is well.

Chapter 7

THE PATH TO GOD

The path to God often becomes a rocky road for gays and lesbians. They grow in their wisdom and understanding of the world, as well as in their awareness of their nature and they quickly see the two are not harmoniously accepting of the other.

An important part of the world's understanding and acceptance stems from beliefs held and perpetuated by the church. Many traditional churches do not yet accept the gay or lesbian for who they are. The parents of a gay or lesbian child have already been taught to believe that homosexual expression is wrong. This gives to the gay or lesbian, who is already struggling with their nature, no support system of acceptance for the way that God created them. For as long as gays and lesbians perceive the church and God as one without the knowledge of themselves and God as one, they are destined to feel spiritually disenfranchised.

Many gays and lesbians who are struggling toward wholeness find it necessary to leave the church. This often becomes an important step in finding God. Those who stay without questioning often damage their self worth through guilt and shame regarding their God-created self.

With regard to homosexuality, it is interesting to note many traditional churches which are Christian are not necessarily totally reflective of the message of Jesus Christ. After all, Christ did not teach that homosexuality is wrong. In fact, he did not mention the topic at all. Christ did teach that we should love God, that we should love one another and that we should not sit in judgment of others: that only those without sins should cast the first stone. Perhaps some of the traditional Christian churches have deceived themselves that they are without sin. They are throwing stones. Have they missed the message of the meaning of the life of Jesus Christ?

It must also be said that all churches are not to be placed in a narrow category which is devoid of love for their homosexual members. Several traditional churches are now trying to reconcile the needs of their gay and lesbian congregation. They are to be applauded for every step forward in this direction.

There are other churches which are and always have been totally accepting of everyone such as the Unity churches and the churches of Religious Science. Gays and lesbians have always felt comfortable there in cultivating their relationship with God. The author's beliefs and the message of this book more closely aligns with Unity and Religious Science beliefs.

It should also be mentioned that there are churches especially for gays and lesbians where everyone is welcomed. The largest and best known of such churches are the Metropolitan Community Churches.

If they so choose, the gay and lesbian of today need not be without a church where they are comfortable worshipping God. The mistake would be in thinking that any church and God is any more synonymous than self and God. At church, home, work and play, the alpha and omega of the experience of God is always a personal one. Development of this personal relationship with God is empowering to all, but especially to the spiritually disenfranchised gay or lesbian, their families and friends. This relationship of God and self will help everyone to experience the love of God within themselves. This realization shall enable them to express and to experience the love of God in the world.

Knowing this Oneness with all there is becomes the profound experience of why we are here. Gays, lesbians, their families and friends are here to experience the love of God for who they are. They are here to teach this love of God in the world through their actions in the world and their treatment of others.

How does one develop this personal relationship with God? The relationship grows in the very same way that one develops any other relationship. One spends time communicating with the other. One cultivates the other. One interacts.

Many fail to realize that communication is composed of two major components. There is the active phase of expression of thoughts or giving, and the more passive phase of listening or receiving. Actually, all truly effective living is but a balancing of giving and receiving.

Relationships cannot grow when only one of the major components of communication is present. There is much visible evidence in the world to support this truth yet individuals are often incredulous about "what went wrong" when relationships end. It is granted that there may also be other reasons for relationships not thriving, but a lack of two-component communication is always also present.

While everyone may implement these truths to create better personal relationships in their lives, they may also use the same truths to develop their personal relationship with God. Two-component communication with God involves the use of prayer and meditation. Prayer is the active component of giving one's expression to God. Meditation is the more passive component of receiving God's expression. Prayer is speaking to God and meditation is listening while God speaks to you.

As is the case with all other relationships, most individuals are a lot better at talking than they are at listening. The person praying says: "God, please give me a home, a car and make me a movie star", and continues repeating this while God says: "Get in your car my child and drive to Daytona Beach." All the while, the person praying has been and continues repeating the thoughts like a mantra: "God, please give me a home, a car and make me a movie star." Got the picture? We do a tremendous amount of talking to God but we often fail to hear and listen.

On some level, most individuals are aware that "God knows their needs before they ask" but this awareness does not yet exist at the gut level for most persons. When this becomes a reality, it shall revolutionize the prayer process. Instead of using it to ask for things of the world, it shall be used to ask for qualities of God, to express thankfulness for God's gifts, and to pour out blessings for others.

After all, you do not have to ask God for things of the world. You can create them as co-creator with God through the correct use of thought in the manifestation process. If you are still in doubt about this, re-read Chapters 4, 5 and 6 for a review of the process. This is the most effective way to create the things one desires of the world.

On the other hand, prayer is best used as a process through which you strive to experience God so that you might be better prepared to emulate Mother-Father God in the world. Pray then to experience the love of God, the peace of God and the joy of God. Pray to experience the wisdom of God and the powerful word of God speaking through you. Pray to become an example of God in the world.

There is nothing wrong with having "a home and a car and being a movie star". The point is you do not need to pray for these things; you only need to create them.

Meditation is the most neglected of the two-component communication process with God. Many confuse prayer with meditation and consider them to be synonymous. They are not the same. Prayer is giving and meditation is receiving. Prayer is speaking and meditation is listening. To have true communication with God which serves in developing your personal relationship with God, you must be both willing to speak and to listen to God. You must be willing to give and to receive.

Being a good listener is usually not a natural ability. One must work at it through practice. Likewise, to be a good mediator usually takes practice. Such practice usually begins by learning to exercise control of the breathing process. Slowing down the breathing enables the worldly mind to slow down it's chatter so that the Godly mind can attune itself to God. It can be compared to tuning in a radio station on your car radio with the space to either side of the band being comparable to the worldly mind. Being directly on the band permits the clearest communication via the Godly mind.

Slowing down the breath slows down the heart rate, brain waves and other bodily processes. These create the ideal environment for meditation, the act of listening to the word of God. Practicing the meditation process eventually enables you to practice the presence of God in all states of awareness. This gives you the ability to always hear the word of God no matter what else might be happening in your world.

This state of "always listening" and "always hearing" is only accomplished through your willingness to act upon the guidance God gives. If God should say, "Get in your car and drive to Daytona Beach", then you must go. You must not say, "Oh, this is just my imagination talking" and therefore, discount the information. God often uses one's imagination to communicate. Being willing to listen to God and to follow God's guidance is prerequisite to arrival at the state of always practicing the presence of God.

If one is not accustomed to talking or listening to God, the process of prayer and meditation can seem strange. It will certainly seem strangest to those who feel devalued by God and to those who believe that God does not approve of homosexuals. You must first get used to the idea that this belief is incorrect and that you have arrived there by accepting the word of man masquerading as the word of God. God only loves and only gives.

Until the strangeness disappears, you may want to keep the application of prayer and meditation a secret. Doing so will avoid the negative thoughts of others until you have developed personal proof the two-component communication tool works in developing your relationship with God.

Homophobia encourages homosexuals to distance themselves from God. The false idea of God's lack of approval keeps them repressed about their nature and in the closet. It is time for gays and lesbians to claim their spiritual empowerment in the world. Changing one's beliefs about God is mandatory. The practice of meditation and prayer are keys to progress.

The path to God may have begun as a rocky road but it does not have to remain so. It may easily become a gravel path, a trail of sand or a brilliant light with no need for distance in between. How quickly one arrives at the light is not dependent on the homophobic world but on the beliefs held and the choices made by each individual upon the path. One can take as long as one chooses but one cannot avoid the journey to the light. The path to God is life itself.

REFLECTIONS

Mother-Father God, help me to develop my personal relationship with You while knowing that it can never be dependent upon any person or any organization. Human authority which does not speak for a loving God in a loving manner is devoid of You. I would have nothing to do with anything but Your truth. I shall seek out persons and organizations which speak Your truth and I shall pray for my brothers and sisters who do not.

Mother-Father God, I value the strengthening of our communication. Through meditation and prayer, You will find me always willing to speak and to listen. In prayer, I shall ask to be more like You and to express like You in the world. As You speak to me in meditation, I promise to listen and to act upon Your guidance no matter how ridiculous it may seem. I know that as I act upon Your guidance, more will be given. Thank You for loving and comforting me on my path to You. I am at peace.

Chapter 8

PERSONAL HEALING: FORGIVENESS IS THE KEY

Gays and lesbians have a lot of personal healing to complete just as do those who vehemently oppose them. While the specific individual motivations may differ, both groups are spiritually yearning to undo an illusionary idea into which they unwittingly bought.

Some homophobic heterosexuals have bought the idea that same sex relationships are sins against God. This belief is irrational and does not serve God because it assumes that not all of God's creations are good. It also assumes God is not a loving God. Thus, sin becomes a false idea about the Son of God, His word and His works as the word "sin" is given man's interpretation.

While the word sin may be given many different interpretations and definitions, we shall use the one derived from an archery term indicating "off the mark". When the archer dispatched the arrow toward the target and missed the center, he would hear the person who was relating the results say, "sin" which simply meant the person missed hitting the bull's-eye. They sinned; they were off the mark.

This interpretation of the word sin might suggest that all homophobic heterosexuals have sinned; they are off the mark in their thinking because they have wrongly perceived God's nature, God's creations and have wrongly interpreted for God. They have simply made a mistake and the error can be corrected. Just as the archer can continue to practice until he or she no longer misses the bull's-eye, consistently hits the target, no longer hears the word sin and no longer is off the mark, any error may be corrected.

The homophobic heterosexuals who have sinned in their thinking can correct their error through forgiveness. In doing so, they must forgive themselves for all of the homophobic thoughts they have held which are devoid of love and distanced from God. They must also be forgiven by those who were the object of such thoughts. They have, after all, merely made a mistake and need only to forgive and be forgiven to begin anew.

What about homophobic homosexuals, how have they sinned? How have they been off the mark in their thinking? They too have misperceived the nature of God and the motivations of God for creating them as they are. What seems apparent here is that God is not to be questioned; it is man's interpretation of God which is deserving of question. What a revelation it will be when homophobic gays and lesbians realize the fears they experience about their nature have been created by their own acceptance of a homophobic God as defined by homophobic heterosexuals. If this were not so, gays and lesbians would accept themselves as the person God created them to be and they would feel loved by God. Their inaccurate belief has served as a barrier to the experience of self love and God's love. Continuing in the acceptance of this belief is the only thing that can perpetuate the feelings of spiritual disenfranchisement which is experienced by many gays and lesbians.

This spiritual confusion among gays and lesbians is well stated by their acceptance of the inverted pink triangle as their symbol. The metaphysical significance of the triangle represents body, mind and spirit, with the upward apex indicating spirit in a triangle which is right side up. Reflect for a moment on the placement of spirit in the inverted triangle; and why, one might ask, is the triangle pink?

The metaphysical significance of the color pink is love. If one interprets the meaning of the homosexual symbol of the inverted pink triangle which has been accepted by gays and lesbians, the interpretation is clear. Love, devoid of spirit, is turned up side down. What is wrong with this picture?

The author suggests a better symbol would be a triangle turned right side up with it's apex reaching for the spiritual heritage rightfully belonging to gays, lesbians and everyone else for that matter. Instead of the color pink, which is reflective of the love of mankind, why not white, reflective of the white light of God's love. Wearing the white triangle on one's heart and soul will allow homophobia to heal.

Reflect for a moment from where the symbol of the inverted pink triangle came. It came from Nazi Germany and Hitler. It came from a man who was an Anti-Christ who identified homosexuals by having them wear the inverted pink triangle and who persecuted them. Is this an image gays and lesbians should accept as representative of who they are? They can only cling to such a symbol for as long as they fail to recognize the truth about themselves and God. God only loves and gives and God is good and so are they. Until gays and lesbians recognize this simple truth, they shall continue to feel and be oppressed for their thoughts must create their world.

All of this "sinning" or being "off the mark" can immediately be undone by gays and lesbians forgiving themselves for ever accepting the homophobic God of homophobic people. Many gays and lesbians have had to throw away this God in order to survive and, in so doing, have deprived themselves of a spiritual relationship. The ones who developed their spiritual relationship with God were able to do so because they realized that it was, after all, a personal relationship not dependent upon any person or organization.

Whatever misperceived ideas gays and lesbians have had, all can be resolved through forgiveness. Each individual must begin with forgiveness of self for being off the mark by believing in a homophobic God and they must forgive the ones who also were off the mark by wrongly creating this homophobic God in their own image. Everyone has sinned, everyone has made mistakes. All can be healed through forgiveness.

Forgiveness seems difficult, and sometimes impossible, because people often misperceive what forgiveness is. Some think that forgiveness means condoning and they simply refuse to do so. Some think that to forgive is to forget and they simply cannot do so. Both notions about forgiveness are totally incorrect.

When someone has done some terrible wrong, forgiving them will not be saying what was done is acceptable. If it was unacceptable then, it is still unacceptable nor will the person doing the forgiveness ever forget the terrible thing that was done. How could this be so? They cannot forget something that is a part of their memory just because an act of forgiveness takes place.

Many individuals believe, because they cannot forget and condone, they cannot forgive. This is untrue because they have misperceived the meaning of forgiveness. Forgiveness has nothing to do with the person who has done the wrong. It has everything to do with the person to whom this wrong was done. Forgiveness is not about "them". It is about you. Forgiveness is not doing "them" a favor; it is doing "yourself" a favor.

Who has been bothered by the fact this awful thing happened? Who churns with emotion every time they think of what happened? Who grinds their teeth at night and has nightmares on this issue? Who is consumed by anger and bitterness? The answer may or may not be "them" some of the time but it most certainly always is "you". It is for the purpose of freeing oneself that one must forgive. Forgiveness is not a selfless act. It is an act of survival.

If forgiveness is viewed from this perspective, most persons can see forgiveness offers everything they want. The act of forgiving allows them to change forever the way this thing continues to affect them. They defuse a stick of dynamite within their mind. This frees them to create a different set of thoughts which create a different reality.

For example, it is not uncommon for a person who has been physically or sexually abused to have this pattern repeat in their life. This is understandable because they continue to hold emotionally charged thoughts on the traumatic event. This acts like a magnet to create another occurrence and so forth. Forgiveness interrupts the pattern by defusing the energy of the thoughts surrounding the event.

Even though it is not usually or primarily expressed in these terms, the forgiveness process is what a good therapist or a twelve step program, such as the one espoused by Alcoholics Anonymous, helps one to do. Individuals who find themselves with unproductive or undesired patterns which continue to be repeated would be well served to see a good therapist and/or join a twelve step program for help with their problem. When all is said and done, the therapist and/or program will help them, through whichever modalities are appropriate, to change the way this thing continues to affect them. This is forgiveness.

Most of the things one needs to forgive can be effectively done by the individual through prayer and meditation. One only need be willing to change the effect this thing has upon them to begin the process. This is enough to be successful as you sincerely ask for God's help and willingly act upon God's guidance.

Forgiveness is important because it frees your emotions of debris from the past and allows you to live more fully in the present. By failure to release the past, you are locked into the "billiard balls" belief system.

When gays and lesbians fail to release the oppressive past and forgive those who have treated them in an unGodly manner, they perpetuate oppression and ill treatment. Their thoughts cannot do otherwise. What one experiences in life is but the extension of one's own thoughts.

Forgiveness will never say this bad treatment was alright to do and the persecutors were right in doing so. It also will not say that gays and lesbians will ever forget the injustices which were done. Forgiveness will change the way gays and lesbians continue to be effected by this remembrance. Forgiveness will permit gays and lesbians to release the past. In so doing, they claim their freedom to create a different future.

What about those who have been the oppressors? The same principles apply. Forgiveness of self and others for the angry and judgmental thoughts one has held has hurt no one more deeply than the individual thinking those thoughts. Forgiveness is the answer and absolution less anger and judgment take their toll on the physical and emotional body and lead to irrational and senseless acts. Shooting a physician in Florida who performed abortions by one who believed abortion was wrong is an example of where anger and judgment can lead. The love of God is not expressed through such behavior.

The point to be remembered is everyone is trying to heal even though it may not always look that way. Gays, lesbians, homophobic heterosexuals are all trying to heal and are doing the best they can even though their choices sometimes cloud this issue. If you will remember this and extend your hand to lift another higher, the world will be healed of homophobia. Forgiveness is the key for all mankind. It offers everyone the things all hearts and souls desire if they would be whole. Forgiveness enables everyone to release the past and to be free to function as a conscious co-creator with God to create a better world.

How does an individual know when they have done all of the forgiving they need to do? "I think I have forgiven everyone. How do I know for sure?" You know by observing the interior landscape of your being. Is the weather stormy and turbulent? Is it uprooting the trees and churning debris or do you find a landscape of beauty beneath blue skies, a warm sun and a peaceful environment? You always know the truth about your extent of forgiveness by the amount of peace you feel inside.

If reflecting upon any part of your past creates anger and/or other negative emotions, there is work to be done in forgiveness. You need only check your peace barometer to know your inner truth and you need only decide how much longer you choose to experience stormy weather. Peace is but the reflection in the mirror through which forgiveness sees itself. Choose then to experience peace through the process of forgiveness.

REFLECTIONS

Mother-Father God, strengthen me so that I might experience Your peace throughout my being. Help me to forgive my past and all the players in it. Help me to see it with Your version of the truth and to heal it with Your love.

Thank You for helping me to release my anger and all of my negative emotions which are associated with my past and affecting me in the present. I now willingly release them to create room for positive thoughts, emotions and people in my life. I realize more deeply how my thoughts have created my reality and I shall, as co-creator with You, create a better future.

I release all of my confusion of the past regarding forgiveness. I see it as it truly is, a way to create peace in my life. Help me to help my adversaries to heal through my example of forgiveness, my expression of love and understanding and my willingness to always extend my hand to lift another higher. Thank You, Mother-Father God, for Your presence in my life.

Chapter 9

BALANCE

Everything in life seeks balance. From the seesaw one played on as a child to the couple in marriage counseling to the balance of trade agreements in the world, all that exists seeks balance. How, one might ask, does one achieve it?

Balance is achieved through the process of giving and receiving. Balance = G + R or equal amounts of giving and receiving. This is absolutely all that it takes to achieve balance in every aspect of life.

A radio must receive the appropriate amount of electricity to give out it's message. If it receives too much, the radio can blow out its' circuits. The human body must receive food for energy and give off it's waste products accordingly. If the giving off of waste is in deficit, the body becomes ill.

To thrive and maintain balance, relationships need equal amounts of giving and receiving by both parties. Too little or too much by either party throws the relationship out of balance. Communication, as already mentioned in an earlier chapter, is itself a giving and a receiving process. If both do not occur, communication is impossible. If both occur equally, one has excellent communication.

You may find it interesting to think of a thousand more examples to prove the theory that balance is nothing more than equal parts of giving and receiving. It would also be helpful if you would then reflect upon the degree of balance you feel is present in your life.

It is not uncommon for lives to be out of balance. This does not mean a person cannot make it from point A to B, but like a car with its wheels out of alignment, the person may be in for a bumpy ride. There are many ways a person's life can be out of balance.

Some individuals may concentrate on work so much that they have little time for their personal lives and families. Others concentrate too little on their work. Both are out of balance. Some individuals allow habits to throw them off balance such as the alcoholic or drug addict who puts everything second to drinking or using. Their total emphasis becomes one of receiving the drug. There is little room for giving.

Everyone, who would be whole, seeks balance but no one who is unwilling to give and receive equally ever finds it. Reflect for a moment on your own willingness to give and to receive. Most likely, you believe yourself to be better at one side of the process than the other.

What kind of things is a person able to give and receive anyway: time, knowledge, love, money? These are some of the most obvious answers. How balanced you are in these four areas gives indication of how out of balance your life is.

Do you only spend time on your own self-centered interests or are you willing to give of your time to others? Are you only interested in acquiring knowledge for yourself or are you willing to share your knowledge with others? What about love, are you only interested in receiving the love of others or are you equally willing to be loving and giving?

Money, or the use of it, seems to be a big creator of imbalance in the lives of many. The emphasis on getting and not giving it stifles the giving process. This restricts the flow of money. By hoarding, one inhibits the receiving end of the process.

The degree of balance in time, knowledge, love and money has a direct relationship with how prosperous one is. Prosperity is used here in the broader sense as the condition of having good fortune.

If you are balanced in your use of time, you will be time prosperous. Those individuals who complain that they do not have enough time simply need to give more of it. If you are willing to both give and receive knowledge, you will always be prosperous in knowledge. You will have all you need whenever you need it.

If you give of your love as easily as you receive it, you will not fail to be loved by many. You will be prosperous in love. If you feel unloved, you can correct the situation by becoming more loving. If, instead of hoarding your money, you give of it freely to balance the process of giving and receiving, you will have an abundance of money. You indeed will claim your financial prosperity.

Reflect for a moment on what in your life is in deficit. Ask yourself the question, "What is it that I want more of: time, knowledge, love or money?" Whatever it is you want more of, give more of it. The person who wants more time must give more time. The one who desires more knowledge must give more knowledge to others. The person who wants more love must be more loving, and here comes the big one: "You mean I have to give more money to have more money?" Yes, this is most certainly true.

Have you ever stopped to think that giving is really all there is. Even when you receive, it is but allowing another to give. Giving is really all there is even though it does not look that way.

Everyone has heard, "It is better to give than to receive", but no one believes it. Most people see it as a platitude with which mama tried to trick you. Mama was right! Just because the prevailing belief happens to be: "I am going to get mine before you get yours", that does not mean that mama's wrong. It is truly better to give than to receive because giving is the thing that insures you will receive. This is exactly how giving comes back to you. Whatever it is you want more of, give more of it!

Most everyone finds it easier to give more time, knowledge and even love than they do to give more money, however, if one wants more of it, one must learn to give more of it. You may conclude the author is recommending 50% of one's money should be given away. If you did so, it would really open the door for a tremendous amount to come back to you.

It is understandable that most persons are not brave enough to try this because, as far as they can see, it would put their bills in jeopardy. If one is serious about seeing if this works, try giving away 10%. If you want to thank God for all your good, call it a tithe. This does not mean that you must give it to a church. Give your tithe to anyone or anything which contributes to your feeling spiritually supported or spiritually uplifted. You can certainly consider tithing to a church if it is your source of spiritual support, or you can tithe to your baby sister if her words or expressions should set your feet on spiritually higher ground. You may decide to tithe to one person one day, an organization the next, and your church the next time. Your decision to place your tithe should be made on where, at that moment, you feel spiritually supported or uplifted. You should tithe as money comes in, less you lose your nerve. The point is to give, give, give so the doors to receiving will open wide. Realize that you are also thanking God for all the good which has come to you and you are recognizing God as the source of your good.

Participation in giving and receiving brings balance to the life of each individual. Each part of the process facilitates and fuels the other. As a person gives more, they receive more. Resolve to emulate God, who only loves and gives, and watch the doors to receiving swing open to accept the abundance which is yours to claim.

Finding balance through giving and receiving is important to everyone but it is especially important to gays, lesbians, their families and friends if they would heal homophobia.

Once they try the process in relation to any one of the areas of time, knowledge, love and money, and they see it works, they may be encouraged to try the same methods with their oppressors. Instead of a defensive posture, they may consider an offensive one of going out to them with disclosure, love and empathy. The same methods of restoring balance will work in healing homophobia. Remember: "Whatever you want more of, give more of it."

The coming out process is important. You must be willing to put on the jersey to play on the team. Coming out precludes healing communication taking place. How can a homophobic heterosexual heal if there is no one with whom to talk or listen?

Communication has yet to begin between homophobic gays and lesbians and their homophobic heterosexual counterparts. This has not happened because neither group has extended the courtesy of listening to the other. Someone must first rise to this occasion for things to change. As gays, lesbians, their families and friends make the effort to balance their lives to the tune of Balance = G + R, they shall have all of the personal strength they need to help the world to heal from homophobia. It can begin right here, right now with you!

REFLECTIONS

Mother-Father God, I shall strive toward balance by choosing You as my role model for loving and giving. I am willing to give more than I have in the past and I know as I do so, I shall open my doors to receive the abundance which is rightfully mine.

Help me to give more of myself by being proud of who I am. I know that You will help me through my fears around this and that my openness will help the world to heal. You can count on me to be brave. Under any and all possible conditions, I shall respond with love and empathy.

Mother-Father God, I shall give of my time, knowledge, love and money as you prove to me that giving means receiving. I give thanks to You for all the good in my life now and the good that is on the way and I recognize You as the source of all my good.

Chapter 10

ESPECIALLY FOR PARENTS, FRIENDS AND EMPLOYERS

FOR PARENTS

All of the people in the life of a gay or lesbian person are significant yet there are no individuals more important than their parents in helping them to accept the person they are. It must also be acknowledged finding out about one's son or daughter is not an easy situation for parents.

They must realize it is very difficult for their son or daughter to acknowledge the truth about themself. They know that their nature is not in the mainstream of human acceptance. They struggle for a long time wondering if it is really true they are gay, thinking that perhaps they are the only person like this in the entire world and fearing if their parents find out, they might reject them. No one wants to lose the love of their parents and so, the gay or lesbian person learns to keep a secret.

For some, the secret is kept for a little while as they work through their own self-acceptance. For others, especially the older gays and lesbians who have lived through a more unaccepting era, the secret is kept forever.

There is no one more adversely affected by the keeping of this secret than the gay or lesbian themself. By withholding honesty, openness and intimacy from the important parental relationship, they set the stage for living a dishonest and closeted life where their relationships tend to lack intimacy. They have learned not to share the whole truth. They have learned not to share their feelings. Unless they somehow break out of this box, they doom themselves to experience relationships which are not as fulfilling as they have potential to be.

Parents can help or hinder their gay or lesbian child in the healing process by how they handle the situation of disclosure. Indeed, if they suspect their child is gay or lesbian, they should gently try to facilitate disclosure if the child appears uninclined to initiate it on their own.

Parents and children must help each other through this process. The sooner disclosure has been handled, the better for everyone involved. The disclosure, or lack of it, will set the stage for how the gay or lesbian child lives their life. It is often the difference in whether or not self-worth and self-acceptance are strong and integral parts of their make-up. If their life is devoid of these very important ingredients for success, their personal and/or professional lives may not approach the level of which they are capable. Coming to terms with who one is and accepting and loving oneself is the foundation on which the successful life is built.

Mom and dad must not blame themselves. What they have done is simply to facilitate God's plan for their child. In this process there is the potential for them, as parents, to also heal. The entire situation is not only about the gay child; it is every bit as much about parents. It is a wonderful opportunity to offer unconditional love which parents do so well.

Everyone has heard the old saying, "You cannot change another person", yet many parents try to change their gay or lesbian child. Many have been trucked off to the psychiatrist's office to be healed and many gay sons have been taken to houses of ill repute to learn about being a "real man". None of this has worked. The parent cannot, by any means, change a gay or lesbian child into a heterosexual. The issue is not one of apparel to be worn like a suit of clothes. It has to do with the very nature of the individual.

Parents have two choices. They can accept the situation and this implies certain considerations, or they can reject their child and lose the relationship. The latter brings about a deep and painful loss for both the parents and the child.

Many parents confuse acceptance with rejection. "Even though you are gay, I still love you son. Just do not bring home your gay friends, do not tell anyone else in the family and let us not ever talk about this again." This is not acceptance.

Acceptance not only means "I still love you son or daughter" but also that you support them completely in disclosure. It means you continue to discuss the problems you are having with this situation with your support system and that you also continue the discussion with your gay or lesbian child. "This is going to ruin your life. What about children?" There is much discussion which needs to continue between parents and child. It is the way your gay or lesbian child handles the acceptance of who they are that has the potential to ruin their life. Parents can help or hinder this process.

Your gay son or lesbian daughter may decide to have or not to have children. Not all gays and lesbians seek out the experience of having children, but some do. Your child being gay is not the end of the world but there are many issues you both have to work through. Being willing to discuss these matters will help parents to more easily adjust to the gay issue. It will also develop intimacy in your relationship through good communication where you both feel comfortable in expressing your feelings with each other.

Acceptance means parents totally support their gay son or lesbian daughter in being who they are. This means parents can share the fact their child is gay or lesbian with all other family members and friends while communicating that this is OK. It may not have been what the parents would have chosen for their child but they are willing to love and accept their children as they are and share those thoughts with the important people in their lives. This, and not being ashamed of their gay or lesbian child, is what is present in true acceptance. You child being gay or lesbian is not a poor reflection upon you, but the way you handle this situation most certainly is.

Acceptance means treating your gay and lesbian children exactly like your other children, if there are other siblings. For instance, when parents visit their grown gay or lesbian son or daughter and their life partner, parents should have no problems with their son or daughter sleeping with their life partner. Likewise, when the gay or lesbian son or daughter is invited home for Thanksgiving, Chanukah, Christmas or any other family holidays, their life partners are also invited. They deserve to be treated as a couple in the very same way one's daughter and husband are treated.

Parents set the standard for the acceptance process in the family. To truly support their gay or lesbian children, it must be alright for the entire family to know what the situation is and to know the parents accept their children as they are. Anything less is unacceptance. This will lead to disintegration and distance in the relationship.

The acceptance process is not an easy one for most parents. When they begin to deal with this issue, they need a support system and they need education. If there is a P-FLAG organization (Parents and Friends of Lesbians and Gays) in their city, parents would be well served by attending their meetings. If P-FLAG is not available in their area, parents may try calling the gay and lesbian community center closest to them for information on resources available in their area. Should this not be available to them, they should consult with the mental health professionals in their town or city for appropriate resources available to them.

Parents need not feel they must go through this process alone. There are many avenues of help available to them. If they choose to see a therapist individually, they should choose one without personal bias against homosexuality. They may be able to learn of such appropriate therapists through attendance at P-FLAG or by association with a gay and lesbian community center. If these avenues are not fruitful, parents should feel comfortable asking a potential therapist if they have personal bias against homosexuality. If the answer is yes, parents would be better served in choosing another therapist. If their gay or lesbian child is also having a difficult time adjusting to their nature, P-FLAG, group counseling and/or individual therapy may also be helpful to them.

The greatest remembrance parents can have at such a difficult time in life is the memory of love which accompanied the process of the birth of their child, if this was indeed the reality for them. The child was gay or lesbian then even though the parents were unaware of it. This was part of God's plan and it never interfered one bit with the love which was felt for this perfect child of God.

Focus on the memory when the first feelings of love for your child were felt and experienced. Know it is that love which helps to heal this moment. Focus also on any belief systems one may have which would preclude one from loving and accepting one's own child exactly as God created them to be. Be willing to change any beliefs which are judgmental and stand as barriers to the expression of that love.

REFLECTIONS

Mother-Father God, I need You now to help me through this time of pain and confusion. "Why Me? Why my child?" I know there are reasons You have which are not for me to question, but please God, help me to accept them.

Help me to understand and accept my child the way he/she is. This is not an easy conversation for me to have with him/her. My response to this moment has the potential to help my child to love and accept themself as they are or to hinder them in doing so. It does not have the potential to change them. They are and shall be exactly as You created them. Help me to always be aware of this.

Mother-Father God, with Your help, I shall overcome even this barrier to love and acceptance of this perfect child which You have entrusted to me. I shall set aside my judgment and I shall only love and give. Thank You Mother-Father God for Your help in healing us and our entire family.

FOR FRIENDS

What difference does it make if your friend is gay? What really matters is how they treat others and how they treat you. The only real difference between a gay friend and yourself is that they experience emotional completeness with same sex relations. Other than that, they are very much like everyone else with some individual differences.

Just as one would not want everyone as one's close friend, one would not want every gay or lesbian as one's close friend. What matters is how much there is in common between two friends and how they treat each other.

If one is lucky enough to have a wonderful gay or lesbian friend, it should be OK to openly discuss each other's status. This can only deepen your friendship to be open and honest with each other. By the way, one should not be afraid the gay friend will want to become lovers with the friend who is not gay. Gays and lesbians generally choose to be with people like themselves for love relationships. Heterosexual persons need not be sexually afraid of their gay friends. As this is more openly discussed among friends, fear will quickly be recognized as unfounded.

Once this fear has been handled, both persons will be free to truly support each other as friends. This might mean socializing together with each other's life partners, discussing one's problems, enjoying sports, remembering birthdays, shopping, etc. Knowing your friend as a gay or lesbian person will do wonders in healing your homophobia.

Most everyone has one or more gay or lesbian friends. These friendships should be identified as such so the parties involved can heal. If you have a friend you think might be gay, you might try facilitating an environment of openness and acceptance. This may encourage the gay friend to freely communicate while feeling they shall not lose one's friendship. This is most likely the main reason why they have not already done so.

If you have a friendship with a gay or lesbian person, you should support that friendship among those who are biased against homosexuality. This is how you may help the rest of the world to heal. By refusing to condone words or actions by others which evidence prejudice against gays and lesbians, you support your gay and lesbian friends. You must remember not to go as far as to sit in judgment regarding those prejudiced individuals less the cure be worse than the illness.

A heterosexual who has a gay or lesbian friend must also examine their belief system to identify those beliefs which do not support what they know is right. They must also be willing to change them. Does their church condemn homosexuals? If so, perhaps they should consider other churches and choose one which does not withhold love and acceptance of anyone.

If homophobia would be healed, the entire life of each individual must be totally congruent. The person's belief system and their willingness to take action on their beliefs is an integral part of the process. Gay friends need and deserve one's full support. The healing of the world depends upon each individual and the extent of prejudice they are unwilling to support.

REFLECTIONS

Mother-Father God, I know You as a loving God of all people and I refuse to uphold anyone or any organization who withholds love of anyone and who sits in judgment of others. I refuse to uphold prejudice against my gay brothers and sisters in any form and in any environment. You, my God, shall be my only example, a God who only loves and gives.

Thank You, God, for my wonderful gay and lesbian friends. Help me to support them and to communicate my love and acceptance of them. Help me to create an environment which is safe for both of us to communicate openly about who we are. God bless all of my gay and lesbian friends.

FOR EMPLOYERS

Employers can be leaders in healing homophobia in the workplace. This must begin by taking a stand through their employee policies and procedures and/or conditions of employment stating firmly that discrimination based on sexual orientation will not be tolerated. This should be done with sufficient explanation to include, not only the non-discrimination policy, but also procedures of warning for correction with non-compliance resulting in loss of employment. There should also be a written employee acknowledgment of this understanding at the time of hire. Supervisors and/or department heads must be encouraged to enforce disciplinary procedures whenever discrimination against gays and lesbians occurs.

Employers who would help the world to heal homophobia must begin by reviewing their employee policies on this issue and amending them to insure that all members of the work environment are protected against discrimination. Education and training on sensitivity to the problem should then be offered to their supervisors and/or department heads. All employees should then be informed of the new policy and appropriately acknowledge it through their signature. Notification of this should be placed in their employee file.

Employers and their supervisory personnel are the only ones who can insure lack of discrimination against gays and lesbians in the workplace. Their work in this important area will heal the expression of homophobia in the work environment.

REFLECTIONS

Mother-Father God, I shall do everything I can to heal homophobia in my work environment. All of my employees will be treated fairly and with respect. Help me and my company to do our part to heal discrimination against gays, lesbians and all persons in the workplace. The things I do with my company are important. My policies help to heal homophobia in the world.

Chapter 11

COMING OUT HELPS EVERYONE TO HEAL

At many places in this book, the author has recommended "coming out" or disclosure about their sexual orientation by gay and lesbian persons. A common response to this by many homosexuals might be: "What I do in the bedroom is no one's business but my own". Basically, they are right, but while being right, they are not free. It is because they are not free that disclosure or coming out is needed. Having to secretly be the person one is, separates oneself from freedom. It also separates the individual from self worth and self acceptance. Only through disclosure will freedom manifest. Everyone will probably agree, it is better to be right and free than just be right.

There are many who believe one must fight for freedom. Is this not the message of Stonewall? For those whom are unaware of this reference, it refers to the time in New York during June of 1969 when gays and lesbians physically fought back against police harassment. It has come to be known as the beginning of the gay rights movement. The author, however, would assert: If one has claimed freedom in one's mind and heart, one is free. There is no need to fight for something one already has, is there? So, where is freedom, anyway?

As long as gays and lesbians do not accept themselves, they cannot be free. The frustration they experience causes them to project these thoughts upon the world. Such an act might be called protection through projection. Once they have projected these thoughts outside themselves, it allows them to own the belief there is something out there to fight. The problem is not " in here"; it is "out there". They have transferred ownership but unknowingly, their name is still on the deed. They have conveniently transplanted the thought into different soil; however, this is no annual flower. The bulb for this perennial remains within themselves. It is one of the most difficult things for an individual to see. As long as the thought continues to be within them, they shall see it in their world. Gays and lesbians do not receive love and acceptance from the world because they do not love and accept themselves.

Going back to the coming out or disclosure process, why would someone not want to disclose? There are many possible answers from many individuals. Without reservation, every answer is always fear-based and candy-coated with a variety of rationalizations. "It is none of their business. They do not want to know. I do not want to lose my job. I would be cut out of the will. They will reject me." A rationalization response to fear can go on forever.

If one reviews the rationalizations presented and any others, for that matter, there will be one thing which is clearly apparent. They all subscribe to the "billiard balls" belief system. The individual rationalizing is not acting upon life but powerlessly reacting to life. Life is acting upon them. The reader will find this to be true about any and all rationalizations to fear-based thoughts.

As the reader discovered in Chapter 5, *YOUR THOUGHTS CREATE YOUR WORLD,* one must move through fear to release it and change the situation. It is precisely because coming out is fear-based that gays and lesbians must do it. If it were not fear-based, it would not matter and indeed, it would not be anyone else's business.

Gays and lesbians must move through this fear to release it for themselves. The act of doing so will allow their hearts and minds to claim the freedom which has been missing from their lives. There is no other way to claim it. Personal healing of gays and lesbians will take place through the coming out process. It will not take place through any other means.

Healing does not happen in a vacuum. One person healing a fear-based thought creates more personal freedom, love and acceptance, as well as more freedom, love and acceptance in the world. Two persons create more personal freedom, love and acceptance and even more freedom, love and acceptance in the world. Three, four and five creates more, more and more. Additional numbers escalate the creation of more and more until a domino slide paves the way to utter and complete change. Life, as one knows it, then becomes transformed.

This is how homophobia will be healed and forever changed from fear to love and from oppression to freedom.

Homophobic heterosexuals are dependent on gays and lesbians to facilitate their healing because they need information which only gays and lesbians can offer. They hold fears and misconceptions about who gays and lesbians really are because they do not know who they are. Knowing who they are will help to begin the healing process in homophobic heterosexuals who have fear-based thoughts about homosexuality. Until there is a vehicle through which to learn, their fears are irrational and unfounded, their fear-based thoughts about gays and lesbians cannot change.

Every homosexual can be a vehicle for the healing of others if they will allow themselves to be. Knowing who you are and knowing you also are gay or lesbian will become the catalyst for less fear and more love, acceptance and freedom in the world. Families, friends and employers are able to support the process but gays and lesbians must initiate it.

To cross a stream, one must take a risk and jump. To climb a jagged peak, one must take a risk and scale. To find God, one must take a risk and trust. To be free, one must take a risk and come out. It is a fact of life that new frontiers are forged only through action and risk taking. The acquisition of freedom is up to each gay and lesbian individual through the choices each one makes regarding disclosure.

"Silence is approval." Parents have often inspired and taught their children with this message. "When you see or hear something that is wrong, you should speak up.

Otherwise, your silence indicates your approval." One may do oneself a service to reconsider one's silence from an approval perspective.

Do not fret and make excuses on why action cannot be taken on the coming out process. If you are experiencing a lack of confidence, re-read Chapter 4. If you are worried about money, re-read Chapters 5 and 6. If you are short on courage, re-read Chapter 7. Carry this little book among your movable possessions at all times. When there is a free moment, you will be prepared. Sleep with it under the pillow. Osmosis may expedite the learning process. It is important to continue re-reading the book until you "get it" and "do it". Why is this important? Because every person in the world with a homophobic thought depends on you: You are the "new beginning".

REFLECTIONS

Mother-Father God, give me the wisdom to see what other people's thoughts, which are just like mine, have created. Give me also the courage to take a personal risk to change my world and the world at large. I am ready to assume my place as a conscious co-creator with You. Together, we shall heal the homophobic thoughts in the world.

It must begin with me. Mother-Father God, I am ready right now to release my fear and to create love, acceptance and freedom in my world. Each morning I shall ask myself, "What risk shall I take today to improve my world?" I know You will guide me to the answer. Each evening I shall review my actions of the day and assess my feelings about them. This will give me the courage to continue to create a better world.

I shall always be aware I am not alone in this process, that You are with me every step of the way as I risk it all. I measure my success by the degree of peace I feel inside after I have moved through fear to find the soul I thought I lost, to dedicate and return that soul to You.

Chapter 12

A NEW BEGINNING

With full participation by every gay, lesbian, their families and friends, this new beginning shall create more love in the world through the lessening of fear and more world acceptance because there is more personal acceptance. When gays and lesbians stop being afraid, the world will cease to be afraid of them. When gays and lesbians accept themselves, they cannot help but project that acceptance into the world. Life is always an outward reflection of an inner condition.

When fear changes to love and self oppression changes to self acceptance, the world shall be a different place. Gays and lesbians will experience this difference in many ways. As they discover they are gay, it will be something they can freely discuss with their parents, teachers and friends. It will be viewed as the individual difference it is. It will be totally OK to be whom one is.

Parents shall no longer worry about their children being in sexual danger around gays and lesbians any more so than anyone else. They will have more information. They will know that gay is not something one is talked into; it is something that either one is or is not.

Gays and lesbians will grow through those difficult years of childhood and adolescence with self-love and acceptance for who they are. They will also have the love, acceptance and support from parents, family members, teachers and friends that other children have. This will give them the foundation to emotionally grow into healthier adults.

Gays and lesbians will feel comfortable in bringing their friends or dates home for dinner knowing their parents and other family members will be cordial and respectful of their friendships. Whether their friends are gay or otherwise, this will not make any difference to them or to their parents. There will be love, acceptance and respect for all.

When gays and lesbians fall in love, they can willingly share their joy with their parents and all of their friends and be loved and supported in their happiness. When love for another develops into that special feeling of mutually desiring to spend a life together, the marriage of these two, emotionally and legally, is supported and accepted by all. Each are fully enfranchised in all spousal rights and responsibilities.

Gays and lesbians will live openly in all neighborhoods with total acceptance for who they are. If they take a walk around the block together at the end of the day, they feel as free to hold one's hand as does the couple next door. If they choose to have children or adopt, the process is as easy for them as it is for all others. No longer is being gay or lesbian significant in the raising of children because sexual fear by heterosexuals no longer exists. What is important is that children are with parents who treat them with love and support their best interests.

Dining out is different. Gays and lesbians no longer whisper. Holding their partner's hand or dancing with them is just as acceptable for them as it is for everyone else. All persons are as accepting of the rights of gays and lesbians as they are of their own rights.

All people now see the passing of judgment on one another as shameful and degrading to oneself. Everyone sees behavior, and whether it is loving and giving, as the standard by which to measure their progress and their Godliness as they continue striving to place their feet on higher ground.

Is this not deserving of one's full participation? The answer can only be yes, yes and yes! This brave, new and loving world will take only one moment more to come about than it takes for gays, lesbians, their families and friends to take action on the ideas presented in this book. It will not be difficult; it will not take long. It will only take EVERYONE doing their work. The beginning has already begun.

REFLECTIONS

Mother-Father God, thank You for allowing me to glimpse and feel what Your brave, new and loving world is like. I shall translate this feeling into thoughts which find expression through action in the world. I am committed to moving through my fears and to acting responsibly as Your co-creator in the world.

Help me to strengthen our communication process. Not only shall I speak to You in prayer, I shall also listen to Your guidance as I meditate. If You say, "Get into your car and drive to Daytona Beach", I shall go without question. I am willing to trust You completely and place myself completely in Your hands.

Help me, Mother-Father God, to become the person I am capable of becoming and to release all that would stand in the way of this noble objective. Help me to love and to forgive myself and others. Guide me in a life of service and know that I give thanks to You, Mother-Father God, for using me as a channel for good in the world.

Appendix

Services Offered Through:

THE GODDESS EXPRESS

Goddess Express
6860 Gulfport Blvd. South # 920
St. Petersburg, Florida 33707

(813) 360-6168

MISSION STATEMENT

The Goddess Express is a service company which dedicates itself to the personal healing of the world's population. It strives to uplift the consciousness, illuminate the mind, touch the heart and emotions, and speak to the soul so that many levels of inner transformation may take place.

Through loving communication, the Goddess Express seeks to create change which leads to wholeness. The message stresses balance in giving and receiving and strives to awaken the heart to love. The Goddess Expresses seeks to *CELEBRATE* all that we are and all that we can be.

The vehicles of the Goddess Express are: management services, programs and seminars; interpersonal interactions; tapes and printed materials; the sponsoring of retreats where people may come for rest, renewal, consciousness raising and personal healing; tithing and the support of worthy causes worldwide.

The overall mission of the Goddess Express is Spiritual in nature and directs itself toward finding peace and prosperity within, helping our brothers and sisters and being of service to the world.

CONTINUE THE DIALOGUE IF YOU CHOOSE:

Dr. Sandra St. John offers individualized educational availability via telephone appointment based upon the ideas presented in THE HOMOPHOBIC HEALER. The caller has the opportunity to ask questions and direct the discussion on issues of interest to them.

The caller should be mindful that this is not a counseling service nor is its intent to function in a therapeutic manner with regard to mental health issues. Telephone appointments are offered as an educational service only and are intended as an amplification and extension of the educational process which the book begins. Before a telephone appointment can be scheduled, the TELEPHONE APPOINTMENT FORM must be completed, signed and received by Dr. St. John.

For information on fees and to schedule an appointment, call: (813) 360-6168 from 9 A.M. 2 P.M. Eastern standard Time.

TELEPHONE APPOINTMENT FORM

I have read the preceding page and I understand that the telephone appointment is offered as an educational service and is in no way to be considered therapy.

I understand and accept that the author/teacher assumes no responsibility for the implementation of the ideas discussed or for any future effects upon the participant. The participant agrees to hold harmless Dr. Sandra St. John and THE GODDESS EXPRESS for any reason what so ever as a result of this service.

Before a telephone appointment can be scheduled, the TELEPHONE APPOINTMENT FORM must be completed, signed and received by Dr. St. John.

Signature_____Date_____
Name_____
Age_____
Address_____
City_____State_____Zip____
Telephone (____)_____

SEND TO:

Telephone Appointment/Dr. St. John
Goddess Express
6860 Gulfport Blvd. South #920
St. Petersburg, Florida 33703

THE
GODDESS

EXPRESS

presents

CELEBRATION

a seminar for

Personal Growth and Development

by:

Dr. St. John

99

CELEBRATION

CELEBRATION is an extension of the material presented in *THE HOMOPHOBIC HEALER* through the seminar format. It is facilitated by Dr. Sandra St. John and was created as a vehicle for personal healing and consciousness raising. This experience is appropriate for anyone who is serious about healing their homophobia.

The experience of participating in this seminar is a very special moment in time, when the message and the facilitator can become a catalyst in the personal healing process. The seminar is offered with hope that the participant may heal, be inspired to live life differently and become a bridge to empowererment in the lives of others.

CELEBRATION celebrates the person that we are and the person we are capable of becoming. The seminar offers both informational and experiential work and is approximately three hours in length. For complete information on the seminar, complete the Seminar Notification Form on the next page.

SEMINAR NOTIFICATION FORM

Please send complete information and notify me when your next CELEBRATION seminar is scheduled. I am interested in attending the seminar in any of the following cities.

___N.Y.C.	___Ft. Lauderdale	___Chicago
___Boston	___Denver	___Kansas C.
___Wash., D.C.	___Seattle	___LA
___Atlanta	___SanFrancisco	_____
___Tampa	___Dallas/Ft.W.	other

___I AM INTERESTED IN ORGANIZING AND SCHEDULING A CELEBRATION SEMINAR IN MY TOWN OR CITY OF _____.

Name_____

Address_____

City_____ State_____ Zip_____

Telephone (____)_____

SEND TO:
    Celebration Seminars: Goddess Express
    6860 Gulfport Blvd. South # 920
    St. Petersburg, Florida 33707

THE
GODDESS

EXPRESS

AFFIRMATIONS
FOR
PERSONAL HEALING

THE GODDESS EXPRESS
6860 Gulfport Blvd. S. #920
St. Petersburg, FL. 33707

Affirmations for Personal Healing are available through the Goddess Express. They contain forty-two affirmation cards and a set of instructions for their use. The cards are the size of a business card as indicated above. They are an excellent educational tool for anyone who is interested in personal growth.

Each set comes with an attractive card holder and in a box for gift giving or mailing. The cost is $9.95 per set plus $1.50 for handling and shipping. Florida residents should add 7% sales tax. See Order Form on the following page.

THE HOMOPHOBIC HEALER and AFFIRMATIONS FOR PERSONAL HEALING are available through the Goddess Express. Indicate items and quantity below.

QUANTITY	ITEM	PRICE PER UNIT	TOTAL
_____	Book	$8.95	$_____
_____	Affirm. Cards	$9.95	$_____

Add $1.50 per item shipping and handling $ 1.50

                                          Total $_____

Florida residents add 7% Sales Tax $_____

                                    Grand Total $_____

___ Enclosed is my check for the full amount.

Signature_____Date_____
NAME _____
ADDRESS _____
CITY_____STATE_____ZIP_____
TELEPHONE_____

Send To: GODDESS EXPRESS
6860 Gulfport Blvd. S. # 920
St. Petersburg, FL 33707

Let Us Hear From You...

We would like to know why you purchased this book, how it has served your needs and the areas on which you need more information. It is the intention of the author to address these areas in future publications.

If you would like to be placed on our mailing list for notification of new publications and seminars in your area or other activities sponsored by the GODDESS EXPRESS or Dr. St. John, Xerox this page, complete the form and send to:

GODDESS EXPRESS
6860 Gulfport Blvd. South #920
St. Petersburg, Florida 33707

Name_____
Address_____
City_____ State_____ Zip_____
Telephone (____)_____

THANK YOU FOR YOUR COMMENTS:

Blessings!